SOMEWHERE, A WOMAN LOWERS THE HEM OF HER SKIRT

Laurie Rachkus Uttich

Riot in Your Throat
publishing fierce, feminist poetry

Uttich, Laurie Rachkus.
1st edition.
ISBN: 978-1-7361386-4-9

Cover Art: Leticia R. Uttich
Cover Design: Kirsten Birst
Book Design: Shanna Compton
Author Photo: Macbeth Studio

Riot in Your Throat
Arlington, VA
www.riotinyourthroat.com

*For the circle of women in my life who pick me up,
dust me off, make me laugh, and pour me wine.*

Thank you for never telling me to lower the hem of my skirt.

CONTENTS

PREFACE

PART ONE: *n. girl*

PART TWO: *n. townie*

PART THREE: *n. daughter*

FOOTNOTE

PART FOUR: *n. mother*

PART FIVE: *she, her, hers*

POSTFIX

PREFACE

A STUDENT WONDERS WHY I STARTED WRITING POETRY IN MY 40s

A few years ago, I whistled for my dog in the Florida heat
and the grandmother I never met stood up from her knees

in a Lithuanian field. She held out a poem in the shape
of a pocketbook and I made it into a soup like the women

who came before me were known to do. I invited
them all in and held their babies while they lifted spoons

to their lips and talked about salt and men and the price
of pantyhose. My grandmother always wanted a pair,

and how do you tell a woman who hid from the Huns
and ducked into America that nobody really wears stockings

anymore? I said I'd try Kohl's. Then the sun turned
and the women left one by one and my grandmother set

her saucer in the sink and dried her hands in my hair.
I threw the poem into a Midwest coal mine, but the canary

sang and the men cleared out in a cloud of black
lung. The poem stuck to my grandfather's boots and he

tracked it all over the tile of the Great Depression.
Before long, the poem smelled like whiskey and Friday

night fish fries and corner bars that ate paychecks, so
I swept it into my son's closet that smells like weed

and missing Algebra assignments. But the poem cried
and, trust me, you would, too, in there. It's all Fortnite

and football and not the place for a poem with a
permanent case of PTSD, so I scooted over a lifetime

or two and the poem came and sat on my lap like a cat.
Tell me: what else could I do, but click off Netflix

and keep it? I rubbed my grandmothers into the roots
of my hair and nodded to my dead mother who stood

in the corner—she brought me a coupon for Kohl's—
and the words lined up like words will when you whistle

for them   and all the women
        I've been leaned in to listen.

PART ONE
n. girl

MATTEL, IN THEIR INFINITE WISDOM, DECIDED SALLY RIDE WOULD WANT MAKEUP

In 1983, *Vogue* asked you what you'd do if you got your period
in space and you said, *I'm hanging up now*, but you didn't. You just

breathed into the phone and waited for 36 years to pass and Mattel to turn
you into a Barbie and call you *inspiring* and maybe that's fine and maybe

I'm projecting and maybe we've orbited past the Johnny Carson
jokes that wondered if the flight was delayed because you couldn't

find a purse to match your shoes and maybe today we would be ashamed
to ask if you'd wear a bra, but I remember being 15 and watching

the space crew's press conference and when some man
asked if you thought you'd cry during the flight, you said, *Why*

doesn't Rick get asked that question? and my hometown fell off
into the sea and something rose in me that's never sat back down.

We watched you somersault through time and when you landed,
you told little girls, *Weightlessness is the great equalizer* and I forgot

all about the makeup kit NASA decided you needed until
Mattel finally wrestled you down and smeared lip gloss over

your smile, lined your eyes black, and made you blush.
Maybe it's not fair that I still zip a 60-year-old Barbie into a prom

dress and countdown her measurements like weather reports, because,
look, they're trying—they really are—and curvy, red-hair Barbie rocked

that *Girl Power* tank last year and she landed in more little girls' homes
than Thigh-Gap Blonde Barbie with the midriff and the microphone, but

damn, Dr. Ride, it hurts 15-year-old me to see you on that shelf, even
in a loose flight suit and flat shoes. They stuffed you into a package

where only a woman fits, and it was always about the job for you.
When you left what the world wanted for you in a trail

of flame, your mom said, *Thank God for Gloria Steinem*, and we all
cheered and it wasn't a cliché to say the stars felt as if they were right

within our reach. We had come so far, hadn't we?

DEPRESSION, MOM'S

You're 100 miles away from that little white pill she'll
finally place on her tongue, the host without the wine, and even

then, some days she'll still be blue, submerged in waters you
can't wade but it'll matter just a little bit less. You'll hang

up the phone, you'll cut college classes, you'll meet boys in ball
caps: John Deere, Sigma Chi. You'll call them *baby* and drink spilt

beer off bars with straws. You'll skip classes except for Professor
Newby's who sweats and says *Subjunctive* as if it's the wish it is.

You'll bring these boys in bars home and turn them into boys
in beds. You'll think you can change him, and him, but you won't

know what that means and, really, you just want him to stop
punching the walls you share with your roommate—I mean, look,

she's running out of Prince posters—and when he says one night
right before you sleep, *you know, you could be really pretty if you just*

tried, you'll whisper *how?* and you'll remember that—only that, only
you—years later, not him, really, you'll never think of him at all. But

when you are small, five and eight and twelve, you still think of her
moods as moments, movements, folds in gowns you could levitate

with arms that raise seams or stop waves. You're no Moses or Mary, but
still you stand at shores, silent and sure *if you could, if you could just,*

you could separate seas, stomp the serpent under her heel. *If you
could, if you could just.* You'd be really pretty if you tried.

A FAN LETTER TO THE GIRL WITH THE "FUCK YOU, YOU FUCKING FUCK" T-SHIRT IN LINE IN FRONT OF ME AT PUBLIX

Baby, I see you in that skirt, plaid with pleats, the color
of Catholicism and shortened with swagger, and I watch you

tug on it while you wait, because you can step into combat
boots and pierce a perfect, purple brow, and you can lift

a curse to your chest and hold your hand over the heart
of it, but you can't make the shame your mama or some

priest birthed in you stand up and walk away without one
last look back. You're holding a Gatorade, a sub, a phone

with a skull, and the attention of every man in this place.
You're in the suburbs, girl, and nothing about you says

I want to please you and these men? Even they know better
than to tell you to smile. Everything about you says *Don't*

speak to me and everything about me—from my heart
tattoo to my flared jeans with the pink flowers—says *Please*

let me help you. I wish we could talk about those fucking
fucks, those men always ahead of us in line, those laws only

they can change, those protests that make us feel better
until they don't. Maybe we're the same kind of mad? I don't

know when I lost the taste for rage, when I stopped
letting it fatten me. But, damn, I love the scent of it on you.

My pen is heavy with want, but did I forget to become
wanton? I follow you out and step into my small,

silver car with stickers that say *Tell your dog I said Hi* and
Kindness Matters and I wonder if who I've become is who I am.

THE COUNTRY EGG DINER: FIRST DAY OF DEER SEASON

It's 4:22 a.m. and cold squats over the cafe, presses
its face into panes and smears Candy and Rhonda and me
into shapes. We turn beans into brew, flip chairs onto floors.

We stand in shadows, straighten our skirts, eye the door. All
the men are here, camo hats and John Deere green, standing
in line like rifles in a rack. Candy sighs, ties my apron tight.

I think I'm still asleep, she says, Virginia Slims in my hair. *I think
I'm still drunk*, Rhonda says, and we laugh until the boss walks
in from the back and nods to the door. *Save them smiles*

for those boys outdoors. We're easy to track and crack, our prints
on coffee cups and bra straps. In a minute, every table
will be tighter than a tick and it'll be *Baby, bring me another*

and bacon crisp. Sausage patties heavy as hearts, potatoes
shotgun sliced and diced and fried in lard. The men will feed
while the deer still dream. I'm 17 and every man's a mirage

of every other and every tool they need to kill me waits
in a back seat. The dark cuts its teeth on the sky and the wind
sharpened for skin yanks snow by its feet and slaps it

onto the street. The Chevy trucks are locked and loaded,
ready for meat. And Rhonda, Candy, and me—
fish in a barrel—circle four-tops like steam.

KAWASAKI BOY

I never think of you, but today
I saw a boy who looked like you: tight
Levis, fresh-cut curls. A shit-
eating grin. And for a moment, I forgot
I'm the mother of teenage sons. I
tucked their basketball shoes into doll
boxes and stuffed them under my bed
and I was 16 again—just like that—soil
in my mouth, heavy with words I never
formed. I was on the back of your bike,
a bright blade of confetti. The moon

was green then and today it sprinkled
dill seeds. Even a dim light can swallow
you whole if you let it. But you know that.
You drove 65 in a 30 and I slid my hand
over your jeans. You called me "sexy," like
you knew what it meant. You were a shot-
glass word filled with tequila, rimmed
in salt and want as only a boy
with a Kawasaki can be. I called it "love"
and who am I to tell me what I meant?
All I know for sure is today the sky fell

from the shade trees and I gathered it up
like a ghost and carried it home.

I NEVER TOLD YOU THIS

but that foster kid, Billy? The one the Baptist couple brought in? The three of them sat at our kitchen table, the man as tepid as tap water, the woman with tea stains on her teeth. I don't know where the hell they came from, but he said *brotherhood* like it meant all of us and she said *Billy* like he was a pet and it was 1977 or 1979 and I didn't have my period yet, just a training "tank" and an Andy Gibb poster I tried not to pray to. You told me to take Billy upstairs—*be nice,* you said—and I had a koala bear with one eye and a Barbie dream house I couldn't yet give away and I thought, *Oh no, please no,* because Billy was 16, a Skoal circle on his back pocket, a chipped tooth. Anybody could tell he hated us all: we were soft, slow, the worst kind of fix-it weak. But it would be more than a decade before I'd tell you no, so I took him upstairs and.

Come on, Mom, you can see where this is going, can't you? I blocked his hands with my own, pretended his arms were as polite as Ken's that bent at the shoulders and slid off Barbie's waist. After a while I couldn't pretend, but he still did. *We're wrestling. It's fun. Don't be a baby.* Let's say it worked out okay. I mean, sure, 30 years pass and I still take the stairs, still take a step back when doors close, but there's no news story here, no future politician or NFL football player who left a little DNA behind in some kid's closet. Just a guy who stole second base and would have slid into third if you hadn't called up the stairs and offered cake. There's no story here. Even

then—*God, was I 12?*—I knew I might bend at the knees, might back off the base, take myself off the plate . . . but that catcher's mitt, Mom? It was mine to hold, corset-tight to my chest. One might win, but it takes two to play. And Billy? He didn't need to tell me not to tell—I was corn fed on the Good Girls' Gospel—and you didn't need to tell me, just a few years later, not to put myself *in those positions,* the dorm key cold in my hand. But I also knew there'd be boys in school and boys in bars and sometimes I'd say yes and sometimes I'd say no and maybe it would matter and maybe it wouldn't, but either way: *brotherhood* would never mean me.

YOUR YEAR OF TEARS

For Aunt Kay

Your year of tears started as tears sometimes do . . . suddenly
and then slowing, the half-step heat of summer
as it fits and starts into fall. The women in our family do not cry

easily, except for me, but I was "sensitive" and a child
and expected to grow out of it. I wept with you the first
time. My mother set down the water-soft tomato she

was skinning, pulled the pot from the stove and shushed
us both as if we were whispering in Mass. *All of this is
nonsense*, you told us again and again as your shoulders shook

and my mother held you and asked you why and you shook
and shrugged and shook and still the tears fell, a cascade
that tightened in my own throat. But then

your tears cleared, the light dust that settles over soil
that's been turned, and my mother made tea and wrote
Tissues on the pad of paper by the pantry.

Days passed—the rows of tomatoes sealed with steam
doubled and we started on peaches—when you
cried again. My mother let the water boil.

After weeks I started to think of it as a season,
something that should be expected, forecasted like frost.
After months I turned and saw your face wet—your shoulders

now still, your sounds silenced, the start of spring—and I set
the tissues beside you instead of pressing them into your palm.
Outside, the peaches hardened, too soon to be harvested, but still

they browned the moment you sliced them. Later—one season, maybe two, maybe just now, today in the heat of my own 40-something summer—I would wonder when you stopped.

PART TWO
n. townie

HOW TO GO HOME AGAIN: THANKSGIVING, 2014

Land in St. Louie on a 757. Claim your baggage, but drop your g's
at the gate—you fixin' to eat now, to pray, to drink—there ain't
no need for fancy talk, "professor." And go on, girl, you might as well say
ain't again . . . It ain't like you don't miss it none, sure as shit you do and, don't

lie, you sit in those faculty meetings sometimes and you think: Jesus, they
would have killed you in my hometown—really, beat that *I'm the smartest
person in the room* shit right out of you, and where you from you don't know that?
And do not mention Ferguson or Brown or black or say well, sure, the lootin's

wrong, but. No. No *but*. It's Thanksgiving, and damn, girl, look at that TV:
see them baseball bats and burned-out cars? That 12-pack of Bud that boy's got
tucked under his arm? Tell me you don't see this ain't got nothin to do with that kid
who done got himself killed. Don't look at your own 18-year-old son; don't

blink at his blue eyes. Don't think about the mama just a few miles from you,
sitting at a table with a plate as white and empty as the moon. Don't
say *Well, they never would have stopped him if he was white*. You don't wanna see
Scott sit straight up, smash his Lucky Strike, tell you again to come on down

to the prison where he works, see if maybe he can't change your mind some. Besides,
Russ just got laid off and he's a vet and ain't nobody going to tell him the black
man's got it worse. You only come round once a year, an orbit that ain't never gonna
change these tides. So no. But kiss your aunt. Watch her as she pulls the turkey out,

her arms thick and heavy as gravy ladles. Offer to mash the potatoes, pull the cork
from the wine. Don't look away when she lifts a bowl from the cupboard; don't
wince at the lone breast loose, the hair just back. Breathe her in, flour and vanilla
and lard biscuits. Remember what it meant to climb in her Ford, claim shotgun

for yourself. Remember how she called you baby, how she said none of this got nothin
to do with you, baby girl. Remember how it felt to believe.

MY UNCLE REMINDS ME THAT BLUE LIVES MATTER

Do you see the Catholic,
   Midwest white, hair like mine,
   hand over a red, white, and blue heart?

Do you see him on his knees
   caught in a skillet, fried
   in farmland?

Don't you know how hard
   it is to flip him?

His edges were browned in back
woods and Budweiser.

His underbelly's medium rare, he's
been cooked in coal, but he
ain't Commie pink in the center. He's

got a brother with shrapnel in his
side and he's got a Ford that runs
on fumes, and my uncle?

He ain't got no time for you
or your fumes that won't run Fords.

So don't you come crying to him
when them boys come for you.

THE RED STAMP THAT MARKS OUR CHEEK

Two fishermen pull my cousin's body out of the brown
river, a wide yawn that empties into the mud-filled
mouth of the lake our grandfather dug during
the Depression. My cousin's socks are still on, his
hands still bound. He rises from the water,
a backward baptism that brings two men
to their fishline knees. He's been missing 40 days.

There's no desert fast—no used-car Satan salesman
serving up all my cousin lost in prison—but
perhaps every one of his sins is now washed
clean? See his body resurrected from the current,
his face softened newborn sweet? He no longer looks
like the man who beat his wife. He's pre- and post-
historic now—his liver, finally, pickled pure—and I'm

just 15, but give me 20 years. Two men will pull
a baby from my womb. I carried him for 40 weeks. Two
tongs tear him loose. And that red stamp that marks
his cheek? I'll know what it means. He's destined
to drown in my DNA. The socks of my mother's
family are still on and I can't kick them clean. But
look: my hands aren't bound. I hold them out. I reach.

I GUESS PTSD ISN'T SOME COLD YOU CAN JUST CATCH

because my baby cousin Dave seemed okay at first. Nobody
liked his new girlfriend, but everybody liked the dog the Army
gave him when they upped his meds, called it *bipolar,*
and gave him an honorable discharge and a golden

retriever. And his mama can breathe again because
first it was Iraq and then it was Afghanistan and then
Guam and nobody knows what the hell Dave
did there or anywhere else, but he's home now—he's

alive—and, well, the rest will work itself out, because
he's *home* and we take care of our own even if the Army
won't and we don't scare when Dave says, *I need
my dog* and leaves a full Jack and Coke on the counter.

Dave always had one foot in another door, a wife
at home, a girl at work. It ain't right to pull that shit
with all the kids he's got, but he's not lying when he
says he loves them all. That's Dave, the boy born

in the middle of 8 kids, the one with curls who loved
us girls best. *My eyes are wide open,* the girlfriend-no-one-likes
tells me when Dave steps outside to be alone with his dog.
She's got 15 years on him with kids older than mine and she's

just what you'd imagine a woman in the military would
be, hard in all the places Dave's always been soft. *He looks
good*, I say, and we don't talk about suicide watch or
the dog or either one of his ex-wives and he comes

back in and mentions something on CNN and I say
Thank God, you're not watching that FOX News shit now
and she says, *Well, just so you know, I do...and I support
my President, too* and she stomps outside to smoke,

and we laugh and laugh and I pour him more Jack
and Coke and he tells me, *I just want you to know*
how much I love you and everything in my kitchen spins
away and ricochets into the place where Dave must go

when the meds wear off, because we don't talk like
that but then the girlfriend-no-one-likes comes back
and the moment grazes by. Still I'm surprised when a year
later I see Dave at a wedding and there's scratch

marks on his cheek and I can't get him to speak to me.
He moved down south, but it turns out everything's better
in Texas except for Dave. The girlfriend we-used-to-dislike
is a shadow shackled to his side and he's found

the weight she's lost. Only the dog's the same, still
wagging his tail and riding shotgun to pain. Now when
she goes out to smoke, Dave does, too, and I follow
in their wake, but it's just me loading words into an empty

chamber, bouncing against a target I can't penetrate.
I gather up all the selves we used to be and I go back
inside where his teenage daughter cries and I can't think
of a single thing to tell her that isn't a lie. *He's still*

in there, I say, and I'm praying his mama's right and Our
Lord can fix it, but there ain't even a cure for the common
cold and there's nothing else to do, but get on a plane
where the Dave-I-knew follows me back home through the blue.

HOLLY HOBBIE ASKS IF SHE CAN JOIN ME IN COLLEGE, 1985

I flew out of the North window on the back of a Sears powder-blue suitcase and left Holly Hobbie in a heap in a corner of my childhood attic, crying waterless tears. I landed in unleavened bread. Three days later, Holly called but I let the machine pick it up. Outside, City Mice from Chicago wore miniskirts, rushed sororities, and snuck Shakespeare into dorms. They flipped up his collar and turned on *Fine Young Cannibals*. I sat next to them in the cafeteria. It turns out there's no "r" in wash.

Later, I listened to Holly's message. I thought of her pecan hands, her lips tight as a stitch, her patchwork dress. Everything about her was wrong. What would she even wear to class? It was impossible to imagine her tucked into a right-handed desk, clutching a No. 2 pencil and carefully printing *God is dead* into her spiral notebook. Her arms were too short to make the sign of a cross. She was a hundred country miles away. The boards back home were beginning to soften, the basement was tugging on its boots. For Holly, every night was a Lonely Ol' Night. Prince winked at Patrick Swayze, two poster boys who stood on my dorm room wall and knew the score. *Could I come get her?* Surely there must be enough room.

One day, I went to a lecture Barbie gave on the patriarchy and the benefits of intermittent fasting. The City Mouse I lived with sniffed. Hunger was weakness. It was cute I didn't know that. I kept forgetting I needed a thesis statement. I failed my astronomy exam. I got a job at a deli that served Brie and cranberry spread and alfalfa sprouts on hand-buttered croissants. That night, I called Holly. Maybe I should come home? She told me a gang of squirrels moved into the attic. They grew new teeth and chewed on my high school yearbooks. They flossed on senior quotes that read, "Whether you think you can, or you think you can't, you're right." They spit the letters out and pasted them onto Ford trucks that circled the VFW I used to work at. They had babies in my oboe case. It was crowded and, besides, I hated it there, remember?

I failed another astronomy exam. I got a C on my first essay where I argued our basic fundamental rights were suffering under the recently passed seatbelt law. George Bush came to campus. I rolled debates into joints and smoked them with boys from Chicago who stamped g's onto their words. I started drink*ing* and think*ing*. On a black and white TV in my dorm room, a limo driver pulled over to ask: *Pardon me, but do you have any Grey Poupon?* I shaved the side of my head and added a third earring. The City Mouse said I looked cute.

Holly showed up past curfew one night. I was officially fail*ing* astronomy. She was hitchhikin' without thumbs, headed to The Limited and then maybe St. Louie. Her braids were no longer the color of hay; she traded her bonnet for a beret. We decided it was time for both of us to get on The Pill. I told her she'd look pretty with a perm. I told her to try the VFW. The men tip and don't touch. She could keep her shoes, but it's gotta be panties instead of pantaloons. It's not too late to learn shorthand. One of City Mice stopped by and snickered at her dress. She told Holly it was the 80s now. *You're not in Kansas anymore.* She said it almost nicely. We both nodded and for a moment, we knew exactly what that meant.

PUT ME TO REST ANYWHERE BUT HERE: A LOVE POEM

My mother always slept on the right
side of my father, so I tuck her next
to him into the Midwest earth and tell

myself *Listen: You never have to come back
here again.* I brush my hands off the Dickies'
pants I'm not wearing, the pair from

30 years ago when I waited tables here
in dime-store diners, and I swallow mercy
whole. It's a November morning, the sky

as heavy as heroin, and I stand on the brown
grass next to my Florida-born-and-raised
sons and study the sea of my family's dead.

Even as I see my father's chin in my youngest
son and my mother's hands that have become
my own, it is difficult to think of time

as anything but linear here where the white
crests of stones shoulder so many of our
names. My parents are the last to die. All

four of my grandparents, every aunt and
uncle I call my own, now call Calvary
Cemetery home. The rock rarely rolls away

from the tomb of this town. My grandfathers
rose out of coal dust. Now they rest above it.
Endurance is our recessive gene

until it isn't. Today, the clouds are moonshine
gray and a priest promises my mother
the eternal rest of the faithful. I am not faithful

to much or to many. Or perhaps I am faithful
to too much and too many. Still, there is little
she wanted that I carry within—but I like to think

wherever she is going I've already been. Here in
the cold, I am a child again and that familiar longing
for my mother rises in my throat. When will I stop

seeing her as an extension of myself? I am always
gazing through narrow windows even as I open doors.
I'll never slip into the empty space beside her

grave. Already I'm thinking of flight and folding
these pants into a suitcase I'll never stop unpacking.

PART THREE
n. daughter

CLOUD COVER

There was a mother who carried two clouds on her back, sisters just a year apart. The mother tucked them under her apron strings and fed them homemade Betty Crocker waffles. In the mornings, the clouds held their breath while they watched the mother and waited. They were young, these clouds, one four, the other five, when they learned to measure the mother's moods in moon teaspoons. They sifted them into soft steel and leveled them with a butter knife. Often, the clouds were silent while they waited. But sometimes they puffed, filled their chests. They stretched the strings, stormy over the last piece of bacon, the Mickey Mouse plate. They glittered grievance-gray and screeched: the missing Barbie plastic shoe the other stole (and probably ate), the dog no one wanted to walk in the snow, the television turned to *Sesame Street* instead of *The Price is Right*.

Sometimes it was too much for the mother, these ceaseless storm clouds. And sometimes, the silent clouds with their wordless weighted wants were worse. On those days, the sky stretched taut. No one could feel a breeze. The mother would shake, a dog heavy with creek water, but the clouds clung. They fed her rain; they swallowed her sun whole. They pushed her back into bed and blocked the light from the blinds. Often she didn't get up until the father came home.

They were always sorry.

On Tuesdays, the mother brought them to the Y and slid them off into a chlorine pool. It was only there the mother settled fully—gloriously—into herself. The clouds raced along the lanes, rubbed worries off walls, scraped the cement skin thin. The oldest cloud grew porous and pale, a part of the water, a perfect sidestroke that would eventually swan dive into a college swim team.

The youngest cloud, her form graceless and slow, did not perfect a sidestroke. She stumbled into college. She stumbled out. She picked up a pen and never set it back down. She learned to speculate, to form the word of her childhood with a soft exhale—De*pression*—and even now she considers the winds the sisters swayed under. Perhaps she reshapes her own memories. Perhaps it's unfair to think of the mother as someone inseparable from herself, a weight they both must carry on and off the page.

Today, this cloud—now not so young—looks at a Florida sky, translucent with time, and understands clouds cool and heat a source they cannot feed, but still she is sorry. She is in her

40s, and still, *still*, she wishes she had been lighter as her mother's child, even as she stands in the twilight, knowing that the clouds are, of course, as insignificant as the shadows they cast. She was always without power. She will always be without power. Clouds may block the light or skirt it aside, but they cannot alter the sky. She knows this.

But on those Tuesdays at the Y, the youngest cloud would rise out of the water and wander into the steam. She could watch the mother more clearly if she rested by the window, pressed her scent into the tinted glass. The mother would swim and swim, her back sky blue. And the youngest cloud would fill, would keep filling whenever she remembered the rhythm of the mother, the arch of her arm, the tilt of her chin, the smile that rose in and out of the water, the lungs that kept on, kept on, filling.

GOD NEVER GIVES YOU MORE THAN YOU CAN HANDLE

(or one of the lies my mother told me)

My cousin Cathy, pills and a pillow, a carbon-
monoxide mattress and a running car in a Minnesota
winter. An Al-Anon list in her wallet. That guy
on the corner, a grocery cart and a cardboard
sign. A Vietnam Vet, just like Uncle Chuck
who left his right arm in a jungle of limbs. Come
Christmas, he'll show the little ones how to crack
open a fifth with their teeth. Clayton, a kid

at school, a shotgun to the stomach at just 17.
Somebody said some girl was to blame.
Aunt Kay, a year of tears that ran without
notice or noise until one day they dried
and she went back to making pies. But
maybe that proves Peter right: *After
you have suffered awhile, He Himself will restore
you and make you strong, firm, and steadfast.* She
made pumpkin and blueberry, just last weekend.

And now Dave's back from Iraq and it looks like suicide
watch is working. Two more months, an honorable
discharge, and he's home with the kids. My mom
made it too, after her "decade of despondency," the 70s
blues she couldn't shake, until the 80s Zoloft

finally slid in. Still, the Bible is full of those who gnash
their teeth and wail at walls. Who stuff their suffering
into sack cloths, who stand at rivers full of blood and wait
to drown. So many of us are plagued with locusts
we can't shake. Even the cross above my bed

bleeds while I sleep. Who knows what another
can handle? Aunt Mary: a mother who buried five
stillborns, wrapped them each in Communion-

white and tucked them into the earth. She was the only one who left God out of it and told us the truth: *That which does not kill you makes you stronger.*

MY FATHER STARTS TO SAY "I LOVE YOU" BEFORE HE DIES

My father used to say, "We do love you," every
time he hung up the phone, a gold star falling
out of his mouth, the "do" tucked tight

between "we" and "love." For a long time, I
thought only of the masculine-weighted "we,"
the sweeping infinity "e" that meant him

and my mother. For a long time, I leaned in,
held my hand out for more; the "I" a planet I
wanted to orbit and own. It was only as he

was dying that I could dust off the "do," lift
it out of myself where it sat dormant, a
response to a question I never needed to ask.

Only then, could I step into its galaxy, study
its emphatic stamp: we *do* love you. The "do"
as heavy as his palm in my hair. The mouth

fills before words sweeten. A lifetime of actions
sway on the line; spirals and ellipses of time
and tone hang in the sky to dry. I could

only see this at the end when my father moved
into the asymmetrical "I"—*I* do *love you*—but
it no longer mattered then. Instead, it only

illuminated all that I had lost.

BATHING YOUR MOTHER: A BEGINNER'S GUIDE

Lift her wrist and snip the plastic bracelet umbilical-cord clean. Feel
her pulse, milk-toast weak; her skin still seeped in hospital sheets. Offer
her tea with a saucer and fill the blue kettle she's had since you were a child. Light
the gas with a match and turn when she calls your name. Feel the weight
of the question before the words: "Will you help me in the shower?" Look
her right in the eye, lock your brown with her blue. Nod. Face

your naked mother, tuck the story of her/self under your own set of sheets,
the ones she tucked you in after she brushed the wet from your hair. Turn
off the night light she always left on. Shut the door of your childhood; turn
to the steam. You may find it helps to try to think of her as a molecule, compound
and neutral; the atomic definition of a person, held together by chemical bonds.
If you can't—if you find her body forces you to look through another door, the one

that opens to a room you'll soon stand alone in—think of water instead. Lift
your palm to the wet, watch how hydrogen and oxygen connect and do their thing.
She's always been the well where you filled; perhaps it's no stretch to think of her
as only oxygen now, to place her in the center, to see yourself as the hydrogen hanger-
on you are. You moved a thousand miles away. You turned 20 and 30 and just
about 50 but still you think of her as something inseparable from yourself.

There's no reason to stop making it all about you now. Think of her loose skin
as simply the covering of vertebrates, the tissue paper she once used to line drawers
and department-store boxes. Sure, skin's an organ, but let's not, okay? All that fighting
and failing that organs do, all that first-to-go kind of *last call* warnings men in white
coats keep trying to force feed you about your mother. So, don't. Besides, *organ's*
such an ugly word, lurching itself from your gut and flailing fishlike on the tile.

And while you're at it, let's not label her breasts, either—there's that *organ* word again—
and, God, she would hate *glands*. She always said *bust* and she says it now, too, as in *Would
you mind lifting my bust?* Think of it as an act of physics, a motion through space and time,
a defiance of gravity. Remember, the greater the distance between you and the Earth,
the smaller she becomes. Step closer. Shift your weight; lift her breast. It's just a mass,
not unlike this shower chair with its gray feet, its colander, slip-proof, solid seat. Wet

the washcloth, raise it to the rash, hospital-raw beneath her breast. *It's from my bra*,
she tells the shower head. *I didn't want to take it off in there.* Think of the lotion you'll rub
there later, the cocoa butter she sent you when you carried your sons, the tins wrapped
in baby booties, the Blessed Mother medals she asked you to pin to your own bra. Don't
think of the times she lifted your boys out of tubs, how she wrapped them in towels warmed
by an iron, the Scottish lullabies she weaved into their sleep, the halo of baby powder

that hung between them like a prayer. Don't think of her hand on their heads, her fingers
in your own hair, the White Linen that's trailed her since your birth. Instead, think
of the chemical composition of lotion, think of all that you don't know, won't ever know.
Watch the water drain, slide off her back, fall from between her knees. Watch
these molecules—once masters of the oceans, makers of the atmosphere—
circle and sink. Reach for her robe.

MISPLACED

Sometimes I count the things my mother's lost
like sheep before sleep. I begin with my father,
but he was never as careless as car keys. One
pair of shoes on the back porch steps. His glasses
in the pocket over his heart. His quarters, facing
forward, inspection-still in Army-green sleeves. I
can't remember him ever looking for anything
that didn't belong to someone else. Who
would have thought he'd misplace himself? But

it was me who said *Don't call the ambulance*. And it was
me who sold off what was left of my mother's
things, who stacked blue plates into brown
boxes, who told her what was best, what came
next. And it was me who put a sign in her yard,
and washed the afghan he died under. I laid
it flat on the deck to dry, his scent washed
hopelessly clean. And it was me who found
every word I ever wrote him, printed
and dated, filed under *Laurie* in a safe without
a lock.

DEAR FACEBOOK (FOR HIRE) "QUIZ" WRITER,

Fuck you. Fuck you and your "What Does Your Loved
One In Heaven Have to Say About You Today?" quiz.
Fuck you very much. I hope my ocean grief rises
to the tide of your pop-up ads. I hope I can still click
on those $64.99 shoes I looked at on Amazon last

week and drown myself in commercialism. I hope
you get a raise. (I need brown, full-grain vegan wedges.
I do.) I'm such an easy target, aren't I? My stroke
awkward and slow. I'll do just about anything
to imagine what my dad might say to me. I'll lick

your bottom line clean. I'll come back for more. And so
will everyone else on your goddamn site. We're all sifting
sand for signs. We're all second-guessing dreams,
tracking red cardinals, finding copper pennies we can't
taste on our tongues. But you know that. I click the arrows

that circle each other like dogs and I click it again and again
even though my dad is dead and he's not talking. (He'd never
promise he'd "protect me from Heaven": he taught me
to protect myself. He'd never say he was "proud" of me: he'd
never take that kind of credit.) But I select Try

Again over and over until I forget what eternity
means and where he ends and where I'm at and I
think of him and I think of you and I know
what he'd really say if he could: "Oh, hon, this seems
like such a waste of your time." I act like I

agree. But I'm drowning in loss. (You know that, don't
you? Of course, you fucking do.) I want one last
conversation—and, sure, we can talk about you,
about your algorithm that orbits obits and your client's
emojis who cry one animated tear at a time—and my dad

can tell me how you're just doing your best. You're just
doing your job: "It's not personal." (He never liked it
when I called people adjectives with nouns: no *capitalist
slime* for him. Just a guy who needed a job.) "But what
about the shoes?" I don't say. And I don't say, "This

is some fucked-up evil shit." (I never swore in front
of him—I won't start now—but, dear God, haven't you
ever lost someone? Haven't you ever reached
for your phone? Haven't you ever seen the back
of a head and thought, just for a minute, that's him?)

Whatever. I nod like I always did when he talked, because
the only thing I ever wanted was to be like him.

THE END OF ANNIVERSARIES

It's dinner time and Norman asks my mother how
long she was married. He asks every night, a line
in a *Kafkaesque* play. If she gets it right, my dad
will walk on stage and I'll whisk away her blue
bib, a concrete image to an aging abstract
neither one of us can bring ourselves to name,
and they'll waltz out of this land of bed

pans and back into the 50s. (Is it selfish to want
what I was never alive to see?) My mother straightens
in her wheelchair; her hand flutters at her throat.
I place a napkin on her lap. She looks at me: "57
years? 58?" I nod. They're both right—it was almost
their anniversary when he died—but Norman
isn't listening and my father isn't coming out
with the soup and Saltines. I run my hand over
the rubber wheel. I slide the brake in place.

IT'S BEEN A COUPLE OF CRAPPY YEARS

My father died first and I cut
black lines into the center of my chest
and buried the part of me who believed I couldn't
breathe in a world without him in it. I stitched the seam
and wiped myself clean, but there's his daughter, beating and beating on the walls.

My mother died next, in fits and starts, each death
a puncture wound without a scab. In her last death, my mother
was no longer able to call my name to her lips and a phone rang in the middle
of the night and a woman in white handed me the rosary still in my mother's hand.

My 15-year-old son filled a water bottle with vodka
and emptied it into the body I grew beneath my breasts and
a phone rang in the middle of the night and a man in blue told me
my son was lucky. Our family dog died, the way dogs do, in a slow bleed
that seeps into every season and floods all the floors. My husband lost his job,
the ways husbands do, and my oldest child threw his cell phone away and flew to Colombia
with a bible and a backpack and spent his nights on the streets telling strung-out men stories
about rehab and redemption.

I opened a bottle of wine and I didn't empty it until last July.

I think I'm forgetting a few things.

I wanted to write a happy poem. Something uplifting. Something that would never
use the words *silver lining* or *sunrise* or *tomorrow*, but something where you
would still feel the hummingbird of hope in your throat. Something
that makes you believe things *are* often as bad as they seem, *but . . .*

Look at the title again. You can see the *but* hanging in the shadow, can't you?
It's been a couple of crappy years, but . . .

the heat returns to your hospital hands   the sea stands ready at the shore,
beating and beating on the walls   one son comes home, another stays
more or less clean, a third learns to breathe   husbands find work,
like husbands do   the river lies next to a path where a puppy
the color of gunpowder runs in the green   and when you
dream—and you do dream—it's not only
your father's face you see.

PLEASE STOP TELLING ME THAT HEAVEN DOESN'T EXIST

because it's hard enough to live in a world without my father
in it and you don't get the goddamn afterlife, too. My mother
is in the sea's mist and she settles into my skin and sometimes
her voice isn't kind, but it's always hers. The aunts I loved
the most watch me when I line my lips and one of them tells
me I don't need it and the other says, "Baby, that's the best
kind of red" and my friend Chris once told me he wished
we slept together back in college, back when two work-study
kids from two different farm towns ended up in the same small
kitchen in a campus bigger than both our hometowns pancaked
on top of each other—back before we decided we'd be better
off as friends—and I didn't feel the same about the missed sex, but
now that he's dead, now that he drank himself to sleep the way
the people we're from are apt to do, I slip Chris over my shoulders,
tuck the teens we used to be into the waistband of my Levi jeans
and carry him into expensive malls and Milan. He likes Gucci
and gnocchi, anything that reminds him he left food stamps behind
decades before he died. He made it, until he didn't. Look. I know
I'm still here and they're still there (or not there). I don't need you

to understand that I can live without people I love
until I can't. I don't need you to scold me about my son's
edible I took to sleep last night. I know we're killing the earth
and the evangelicals don't give a shit, but they'll still be the ones
hogging the buffet table in a Heaven I'd never be welcome in.
          But fuck it. I'm going anyway. I'm sitting next to my dad.
He's lifting his chin to the ceiling, leaning in to hear whatever
I've saved up to tell him next. I'm playing cards with my aunts.
I hold two aces in a sleeveless shirt. I'm wearing red lipstick
or I'm not. My mother calls my bluff. Outside, the ocean
exhales, the sound rising from deep in its belly. Chris steps
out of the sea after scuba diving. There's no plastic anywhere.
I hand my father-in-law some Lemonheads. Brown Jesus stops
by and says everything's okay, the way you do when it is

and when it isn't. No tree is on fire. No city is underwater.
All my dogs are here, but my sons and every student I've ever
loved—and I've loved all of them, even the ones I didn't—
are doing what they do on earth, but happily, each one
of them carrying the silver dollar weight of their worth
in the warm palms of their hands. Listen. You go right
ahead and settle into the earth's indifferent dirt. But me?
I'm headed to the beach with a chair that will never rust.

FOOTNOTE

DEAR VONNIE—

Lately, I've been feeling like your student Julie, a walking
wound. I'm always at the community college I never went to, clutching
a notebook to the flat chest I don't have, apologizing. I'm side-
swiping mirrors. I want to do everything right. I pant. It's all very
Nancy Drew, but without her pencil skirts, red convertible, annoying
confidence. (Would I think that confidence was annoying
if it was Nathan Drew? Ugh.)

I wish I could see you after class and ask you how to write
a "college-worthy" introduction. Who the fuck knows? What does
that even *mean*? Google doesn't have any of the answers I want. Is
it easier not to believe in ghosts and God, Vonnie? I'm always
checking my own pulse. I'm not going to write about my mom.
Wasn't Nancy Drew's mother dead, too?

I want to meet your ex-drug dealer's mom. I want to try
on all her wigs. I want to pat that pineapple updo like it's an ass.
Do you think she's still alive? Are you still off Fakebook? I think
we should get matching tattoos. Something small. Is that weird?

The other night, I was walking with a few people, and we saw
a tiny, dead bird on a bench. I don't want to describe it
in a way that makes it sound beautiful or tragic or both. Let
me just say, we saw the bird and the night bent to its knees
and a man I was with picked the bird up like a prayer and we
followed him silently off into the dark, this procession
of poets in long lines like minutes

and it's not that I wanted you to be here, exactly, but
I wanted to send you a piece of the night and the burial
of a bird that silenced our stupid selves, even if
it was just for a moment.

xo,
Laurie

PART FOUR
n. mother

DEEP ENOUGH TO DROWN IN

My blonde, blue-eyed boy is already taller than me at just fourteen, his shoulders wide, his teeth white and perfect. He spent last summer making a fishing rod and he cuts up the minnows he catches for bait. He doesn't blink. He slices them in the center, eases the sharp point into a soft side. Sometimes, if they are small, he leaves them whole, the hook a heel that traps them beneath the heart.

He does not watch their eyes, these fish he catches. He does not study the stutter carriage of their chest or the open-mouth gasp that lingers on the line. Instead, he arches the rod, flings it far with the snap of his wrist. His eyes settle on the space between what he has and what he wants.

I stand at the shore and I watch him. How easy it would be for this world to shape this white boy of mine. To serve up all of his desires, a wide net of want we've told him he deserves. The water before him is deep enough to drown in. And I see clearly now, perhaps for the first time, all of the shapes of bait that dangle on a line in front of my son.

Today, the light settles on his hair and we look out at the sea before us.

Tonight—and the next night and the next—we will all eat the fish he catches.

MY SON TELLS ME HE'S THINKING OF JOINING THE MILITARY

You say *military* like you know what
it means, the word meaty in your mouth.
Mil slides soft into *il*, like milk. Not mom,
which begins and ends too soon. Besides,
the vowel's all wrong. *Itary* marches
in, salutes and stands at your command. But,
then there's *maybe*, another *m*, a long
a cut short—but it's late and doesn't pass
inspection in its wrinkled shirt and scuffed-
up shoes. And who can blame this Middle
English modifier—*it may be*—that showered,
shaved and showed up first, perhaps, for
France during that war that lasted just a
hundred years? It might be good, you say.
One last *m*, a rhyme with fight. And then,
a hard, two-punch *g*. Like gun. Like gone.

A PRAYER FOR MY 17-YEAR-OLD SON ON THE OTHER SIDE OF THE DOOR

Let me flatten my soft spots, roll out
my breasts like batter dusted with flour. Let me

press down on my pointed, mothered parts. Sweeten
my edges until I cut like butter. Knead me into a shape

as thin as time and slide me under his door. Let me
rise like dough. Let me mist into the air he breathes. Let me

settle within him. Let me slip into spaces he locks
and let me leave my tracks all over the floor of his secrets.

Give me the passwords to his silences and let me grieve
beside him. Turn my womb into water and let me swim

in the sea of all I'll never know. Let me be still.
Let me stand at the mouth and watch what he won't let me see.

And then, let me tuck a piece of this wet love of mine
into the cave he's come to call home. Let him feel its throbbing,

rose quartz weight. Let him taste the burnt offering imprinted
on his tongue at birth. Let him remember all his eyelashes

have names. The word *beloved* belongs to him. Oh, God—
just for today—let me be enough.

THOSE LAST MOMENTS BEFORE DAWN

tick in time to the heart in your throat; they slide down soft
ice caps, settle into cups that leave circles on the nightstand. They bare
their Tasmanian teeth and howl, all of them red wolves, California grizzly-styling
their way into extinction while you watch and wade in water up to your no-good college-
degree knees like those polar bears alone on late-night TV. Those last moments before dawn

are just getting started. They roll up their sleeves and flex their sleepy biceps, sharpen
their teeth on your sons who sleep with secrets tucked between sheets you still need
to clean. They replay the message from some sister of Siri who called again to say,
A student in your household was absent from periods four, five, six . . . and they track
that boy in a pack and follow him to back seats, back streets, back doors that might block

his own no-good college degree. They whisper maybe it's weed or speed or some
girl in cutoff jeans and they circle the ceiling and land on your mother who died
alone and they follow you into the Land of What Might Have Been and hover
over The One You're In and you think Canada's too cold and you realize
you don't know *exactly* what democracy means, but those last

moments before dawn damn sure do and they'd like to
know just how the *fuck* can you sleep when 545
parents can't be found and kids are in cages
and what exactly are *you* doing to help
just one out and it's been months

since George Floyd, but now it's
Walter Wallace Jr. and don't
forget, your favorite
cousin wrote on
Facebook
just last
night
All
Lives
Matter

and

Yes, you tell Those Last Moments
Before Dawn, *Yes*. But you turn your
head to the window where the sky lightens
while you look and a bird you don't recognize
splits the silence with a sound that can only be a verb
and the cat you don't particularly like settles onto your feet
and a man you love sleeps beside you on Oprah's favorite sheets
and somewhere an Artic tern finishes her circle around the world and
you remember you could read a book every day for the next 30 years and
there will still be stories behind closet doors in rooms you've never wandered

into and you think of all you don't know, won't ever know, and, God, what a gift
it is to live in a world where wonder bubbles under every surface and look! Right now
two people are touching, their hands speaking in a language you've never heard and she is
laughing, maybe, her sounds rising and falling while the other studies the curve of her chin as
if it's something holy, and you can tell—just by looking—that jasmine could sleet
from the sky or stars fold into stairs and none of it would surprise them.
The world's beauty kneels before them.
                         You can see it, right?

I THINK I'M TRYING TO TELL YOU I SORT OF LOVE ORLANDO

I live in a yellow house with a red door and a front porch with a water fountain on the wall that overflows with frogs and a fire pit my husband built a brick at a time and inside are turquoise chairs and a grass green couch and two years ago I painted the kitchen dark pink and all of the testosterone in the house sat down and my middle son said it didn't suck and sometimes when the lights are on and I'm outside on the back deck, I look in and count all the books like stars and a shirtless boy wanders into the kitchen and a cat climbs onto the couch and the air is full of mint and basil and the steady beat of a Florida backyard that's always just a little bit too much alive and I think about how everyone in Orlando is from somewhere else and I watch the sun look over its shoulder to study a sky that shouldn't be that blue and it is all I can do not to sink to my knees and press my forehead into the heat of the concrete and weep for all that I have.

And, honey, I know what you're thinking about me and my suburb life and, good Lord, how can I be so complacent here in the City Beautiful where some guy drives down both lanes in a big-ass truck with a Confederate flag the size of my car and an alligator pulls a 4-year-old into a lake and some woman whose kid went to school with my kid posts on Facebook, *I hate these parents that turn off their brains on vacation and make Disney look bad*, and a sinkhole rises up through the asphalt we slapped over a swamp and turtles are buried alive under sidewalks in subdivisions most of America can't afford and, God, let's not talk about the cost of food or minimum wage or how The Happiest Place on Earth is in one of the Hardest Places for People to Pay Rent and, Jesus, I don't want to think about Pulse or Trayvon or The Villages where batshit crazy old people have parades and shout "White Power" while riding their golf carts over Seminole burial grounds and yesterday it was 104 degrees and the prisons here don't have air conditioning and the men I write with on Fridays bribe the guards to let them sleep in wet clothes and all of this was before COVID-19 and the warden won't release any numbers but some reporter says over 75% tested positive and that makes me think about Marco who works in the infirmary there—I think he's 50?—who always tells me when I'm blue, "Oh, girl, you don't got time for this."

I was 15 when I first knew my time had run out in the Midwest and eventually I left my hometown where everyone looked the same and moved to Denver, a city the right shade of blue, and I lifted a wine glass to the West and tucked *I'm a Progressive* into my pocket and only sometimes noticed everyone still looked the same and then I landed in Orlando and I've been here for a decade or two and, honey, there's not one thing you can tell me about Florida that I don't know, but damn, if I don't also know everywhere you can go to hear someone read or sing or hold a sign or wear the right shade of blue mascara on the "wrong" face and it's not new to me any longer, but still when I walk on campus on my way to work and I see everyone who doesn't look or love or talk like me just for a minute I forget about every system that's set up for them to fail and how much work there's left to do and, right then, just for minute, hope bubbles up in my chest like the American Dream and it's all I can do not to burst like the bloom of a Florida bougainvillea and rub its scent into my wrists while I cover all of our fences with its big pink blossoms . . . and just for a minute, I swear, I swear it's true, I don't even see its thorns.

BE CAREFUL AND OTHER THINGS YOU SAY TO YOUR TEENAGE SONS

You slid them out of the space beneath your heart, and the person
you used to be followed them out into the cold. You've limped
after them ever since, but the grass grew to your knees and your heels
got stuck in the soil. You track all over the floor of their childhoods. You
can't get clean, no matter how many times you click your heels together.
Home is where they are, and they are everywhere and nowhere now.

Tonight the water boils on the stove and all you can do is watch
the steam rise. There are 190 calories in a strawberry PopTart,
but there are too many ways to die to count. You checked off electrical
outlets after they turned 5, but Laura's friend's kid jumped in the same
lake your son fishes in and he died last summer when an amoeba
swam up his nose and ate his brain. Somehow that mama is accidentally

still alive.   The moon swallowed the sun, but here we are, slipping
a quarter into a shopping cart at Aldi. Your first son learns to drive a car, then
the second, and finally, impossibly, the third and you say

be careful and you say *condoms don't*
always work   and you say *where does Jack's dad store his guns?* and you say
drunk people can't give consent and you say *Jesus Christ, you don't use kerosene to start a fire*
and you say *Emily died the day before Thanksgiving*
        and you say *fentanyl* and you say *she thought she was just buying weed*
            and you say *her mom was waiting for her   they were going to bake pies*
            and you say *drugs can eat your brain*   and you say
                Are you listening to me?   Are you?

and you say *you need a life jacket* and you say *whose boat is it again?*   and you say
when you're in Colombia, pretend
you're Canadian   and you say *why*
are you texting me if you're driving? and you say *Uber*
and   you say
Parkland   and you say
Pulse and you say

what? Texas now? Jesus, how many?
        and you say *be careful   be careful   be
careful   God, please*
be
careful.

MY 18-YEAR-OLD SON MAKES A SERIES OF SELF-DESTRUCTIVE DECISIONS AND I BLAME MYSELF

for Mark Pursell

and my friend Mark texts me and says, *Look, Mama, you left everything
you had on the table and if he didn't pick it up, that's not your problem* and I
nod and sip the drink I won't let myself have and I text him back, *I*

really, really tried . . . like more than I ever tried to do anything. We both hate
hyperbole, but that doesn't make it less true. I hold all I wanted
for my mother self on my tongue, a tiny silver dollar Eucharist

that still sticks to the roof of my mouth. I weigh my worth against
my son's mistakes while Mark says, *I know you tried. And I feel like you
gave away a lot of yourself in the process.* I want to pretend I don't

know what he means, but I see my pen on pages left uninked.
I carry my sons on my back like blame; I tuck them into white sheets
beside me. An alarm goes off in another room, but I am never asleep.

I am shaped by my sons in more ways, perhaps, than they have been
shaped by me. I search the porch of their childhood, but I am
primarily looking for my own shadow. It would be easier to put

myself and my sons in a box and wrap the past in a bow. But how
can I not hold the years up to the sun and study all the moments
I might have missed? *Mama, you have truly done the most you could do*

for these men. It is simple, maybe, for Mark to absolve me, to sweep
through all those years and pat my worry down flat. I love my sons
the way Mark should have been loved when he was 18 and his mother

prayed for him to return to something he never was. I only know this:
I want to be who Mark might think I am, the parent of the promised land,
my heart a mountain a boy becoming a man can rest in. But I am

instead a woman emptied and untethered, a field with a yield
still out of sight. *You know he's going to be okay*, Mark texts as I slide
into bed. *You know he's going to put good energy into the world.*

And I do. For one glorious minute—even as dawn looms light
years away from where I wait—I know.

I KNOW IT'S A PANDEMIC AND IT FEELS LIKE THE WORLD IS ENDING, BUT CAN I JUST TALK ABOUT MY DOG FOR A MINUTE?

We sit in the pocket of a plasma pause, where
every cough weighs the same as a grandmother's
heart and politicians try to decide who to place
on the altar of Wall Street while my teenage

son sits in front of screens and assassinates
men who wear turbans and calls it entertainment.
Everyone here is so goddamn sick of all I have
to say, especially me, so I water a garden full of dead

plants while my husband goes out to buy tampons
and vodka. Inside, a dog who has followed me
through every room for over a decade stays
in a corner, his food untouched. I'm trying

to be poetic about this. I'm trying
to remember the arc of a story, to thumb
a narrative's strings until it arches forward
and sticks into the soft underbelly of some

truth I don't know how to name. All I know
is this: I carry my companion out
into the yard and back again and we do not
speak of his shame at the wet floor by the door,

the tail that lifts and falls like words caught
in a throat. Outside, the roads empty
while my parents rest in graves. The bullets
ricochet out of my son's bedroom

and a friend texts me: *How is Dino today?*

THE MOTHER PACKS UP HER YOUNGEST SON FOR COLLEGE WHILE THE FATHER TELLS HER HE CAN'T WAIT TO HAVE SEX ON THE KITCHEN TABLE

and she shrugs and thinks about the slick back of the ceramic tile, the countless
dinners with chipped plates and shirtless boys and plastic cups with Publix
lemonade and she wonders how she ended up here, still orbiting this Three Boy

Planet, still calling it *Home*, even as its extinction hovers over the horizon.
She sighs and slides hoodies off hangers, stuffs t-shirts into Adidas duffle
bags. She tucks extra-long twin sheets into tight squares and wonders if her

son will wash them. She thinks about the used mattress he'll sleep on and then
about a girl who might leave her scent on the North Star of his pillow.
But the father is talking about phone chargers and how now they'll never again

sink into the Black Hole of stolen and then lost items. They'll stay right where
the mother and father leave them. *Isn't that great?* The mother realizes she's always
thought of her sons as if they're tethered to her and they're bobbing along

in those bubble-wrapped astronaut suits, defying gravity, sure, but one umbilical-
cord yank could bring them home. She made them the center of her life, but
she is not the center of theirs. She spent years pulling her sons close, keeping them

safe from the inky unknown. But today she realizes she's always been the flash
of white in the black, the climax in the movie where the spacewalk goes wrong
and the audience watches as she spirals into that deep, silent pocket of space.

Her sons may be leaving, but she is the one unmoored, oxygen-less, a childless
mother. She's always dreaded this day, always known what she had is as much
a miracle as mirage. But tonight she's thinking about stars and all those light–

years between us and them and she knows even if she stepped outside, if she
threw her head back into the black, she'd only see what used to burn and swirl.
The only thing that travels faster than the speed of light is a son leaving his mother

and a mother shaping into something she no longer recognizes. The father
mentions Aruba or Alaska and the mother pulls a poster off the wall and rolls
it into a telescope. The constellations she won't step outside to see can't lead her home.

PART FIVE
she, her, hers

TO MY STUDENT WITH THE DIME-SIZED BRUISES ON THE BACK OF HER ARMS WHO'S STILL ON HER CELL PHONE

Oh honey, you can text him, you can like his meme, you can
follow him on Twitter and to Target, you can ride shotgun, hold
his anger on your lap, pet his pride, be his *ride or die*. You can
wear those jeans he likes. You can discover Victoria's
secret, buy a bra with a mind of its own. You can
recite *I'm sorry* like it's a Bible verse and Snapchat the shit out

of those purple roses he bought you at Publix. You can try
every one of Cosmo's *30 Ways to Give an Ultimate Blowjob*.
You can remember the name of his mother, his best friend
in 2nd grade, the lunchroom lady who gave him extra
chicken strips on Tuesdays. You can grow out your bangs, toss
your hometown over your shoulder, sleep facing North
with your cheek in his back.
   You can strip yourself for parts. But, baby,

it still won't be enough. You can love him, but you can't pull
his story out of the dark and slide your arms into it. You can't
wash it and lay it flat in the sun to soften. You can't
hold his face in both of your palms and watch tomorrow
bloom from the sheer wanting and waiting of it. It doesn't
matter if his daddy talked with his hands or his bloodline
is marinated in booze or his mama loved his brother best.
   You can't fix what somebody else broke.

   So, girl, put down your phone and pick up
your pen. Take a piece of the dark and put it on a page.
Sylvia Plath waits to wash your feet. And look,
Virginia Woolf has built you another room and painted
it pink. There's a place for you at the table. Sit next to me;
I got here late. Oh, baby, don't you feel it? You were knit
for wonder in your mother's womb.
   You were born for the driver's seat.

I THOUGHT I'D TEACH MY POEM TO PLAY GUITAR

but I never learned and Marty Music on YouTube
                    is starting to annoy me.   He only wants
                                            to teach my poem
            about a horse with no name
                    and a horse with no name
                                    is as ridiculous as a poem

                with pink curlers   and my poem
            spent a semester following Marge Piercy

        and *those hands you love to touch*   into every dark
                            parking lot of Reagan's 80s, and   my poem
                                    is nobody's goddamn fool. My poem

            is Woke as Fuck. (My poem
    should probably stay off Twitter.)   I took my poem

down to the prison   and we talked about other peoples' poems
        and banned books   and how injustice feeds   off

the abstract and we lifted   words like   *illegal alien*   and   *thug*   and   *crackhead*
        to our lips   and we licked them clean   and spit the poison out.

When it was time to write, my poem
        got all shy   and choked
                on its own unimportance, but Marco loves
                                        everybody's poems
                                especially his own, and he says
            my poem
                    ain't got time for that.   And Marco knows
                                        too much about time, so my poem
            slit its guitar strings and used them to floss its teeth   and now   my poem

writes poems
    about horses and

        all of them have names.

BABE, WHAT IF I SAID NO WHEN YOU ASKED ME TO DANCE?

What if I took in those corduroy OP too-short shorts,
that Long Island Iced Tea in your hand, those shoes
that belonged on a boat off a coast of a city I thought

I'd never be able to visit? And what if I said, *City boy*,
to my sister in a way we always did when we spotted
(and dismissed) something so far from home we couldn't

trace its compass back to who we were? I said it that night,
too, but the words were lighter and even though I shook
my head at you—so young, so cute, so utterly Chicago

clueless—I said yes because the Boulder sky showered
me with stars and I was here, finally, in a town where I
thought maybe I could write a poem on my shoulder

and someone might lean in to read it.
        And so I said yes and I said yes and I said yes and

now, here we are, 30 years in the Milky Way between who
we've become and who we might have been. And look!

These three boys of ours—brought up out of the earth
and shot off into a world I'll never be sure of—stand
at the shore of whatever comes next, long-limbed comets

that ink our skies into the brightest corduroy white.
And here I still am, a 20-something girl with a PBR draft
in a plastic cup, standing at the edge of a dance floor

watching you, weighing both of our worths, and wondering
what might happen if I keep saying yes.

IT'S FRIDAY AFTERNOON IN A FLORIDA PENITENTIARY AND THE MEN READ POETRY

and Ronnie says Robert Hayden got
it right, a whipping be like that—"the face that I no longer
knew or loved"—damn, that's it, right there   and
Ronnie doesn't blame his mama for beating him so bad, but
maybe she could have kept her pipe in the car and then maybe
he never would have ended up in a foster home and maybe
if he hadn't been sucßh a pissed-off little shit-ass runt, maybe
they would have put him in a house with a mama who liked kids and maybe
then his foster dad wouldn't have put his hands on him and made him run and

Dwayne doesn't care what anyone thinks   Maya Angelou is the world's
best poet—yeah, I said *world*—and "you may kill me with your hatefulness"
ought to be the slogan for every CO in this shithole, but still like air Dwayne's gonna
rise   he's just praying his mama don't die before he gets out   and he still thinks
if he would have gone to his brother's funeral when he was nine, then maybe
he wouldn't have started crawling out the window at night looking for him and maybe
this is nuts, but for the life of him Dwayne can*not* remember anyone telling him
that Scotty died, but they must have, right? and

Julio thinks Pablo Neruda's got it wrong   just because your wife forgets you
just because she writes, *You know I can't be alone*   just because she sends your letters back—
return to sender? what the fuck?—just because another man's sleeping in your goddamn bed
don't mean you forget her   "I shall stop loving you little by little" too?   I'm telling you
straight, it don't work like that and

RJ's new and he doesn't want to read anything, but can he just say something?
He sold drugs. He regrets it. He has accepted the Lord as His Almighty Savior.
He regrets it, okay? Okay. Thank you.   Marco tells him   son, this here's a poetry class
and RJ says, well, shit, I thought it was that accountability class we get credit for
and we laugh and laugh and RJ says he likes what we're doing over here
better than that chapel with all them white women, no offense, and their bibles and gold
crosses and, Jesus, the men are even worse, the way they look at you like a bill
they gotta pay, but these are the only two damn places with air conditioning
and we all agree it's hotter than shit, and animals in a goddamn *pound*

are treated better and then I read Tim Seibles's "First Kiss" and the men
place the words of his poem on their tongues like communion
and we are all fifteen again, holy and hungry, standing under
a porch light while the earth splits beneath our feet and
every door softens into a window and we don't move

or speak because Tim's words are still alive in
the space between us and beauty crumbles
when you try to catch it—we all know
that—so we let it settle on our skin
and hold our breath until Marco
says, like a prayer,

It be like that. It be just *like that.*

I WANT TO STEP INSIDE MY DOG'S DREAM AND KICK YOUR ASS

Listen, you prick: That dog you had? The one with the freckles
on her nose, the legs that curve like commas when she sleeps?
She's thinking of you again. She's running in her dreams, hauling

ass, and I watch her twitch on the horizon of a white sheet, the past
dented into the black pads of her paws. She makes a noise like only
a woman would, a whimper caught in her chest, a secondary,

afterthought of a sound that knows not to count on the mercy of men.
It's one she's never needed in this house of boys and brawn. I'd give
anything to bring my most aggressive son into that space where you

shifted who this dog could be into who she is. But even in my dog's
dream, I can't make you sorry, can't crack the cage of your ribs
with the toe of my boot without another man beside me. I can't

make you fear me. I can't show you how it feels to be the one who
watches and waits and carries somebody else's crime into the backdrop
of a dream that keeps on keeping on. Once a student asked me

what superpower I'd possess, and I thought about it for days until
I came back and told him I wanted the power to inject empathy, to slide
a silver bullet shot of knowing into a vein of a man who needs

to be strapped down to become kinder. I meant it, and most of the time,
I still do. But tonight, I just want to stand beside my dog as she lifts
the black lips of her broken teeth and everything soft in her stiffens.

I want to taste the crunch of your bone on her tongue. I want to watch
your eyes widen in recognition. I want to stroke the silk of her ears,
whisper *Good dog* into her neck as I sponge your blood off her chin.

I want you to beg her to stop while I stand beside her, the leash loose
in my hand. I want to pretend the scent of my rage is different than yours.

DEAR OFFICE MANAGER AT ORLANDO BREAST CARE CENTER

There's a goddamn lump in my breast, okay? But whatever.
Look around. There's a goddamn lump
in every body's breast   or there might be   or there was and now
there's no breast left; it's erased,
       a dinner plate scraped clean, the fork screeching . . . *can I take this?*

Sorry, weren't you done? or, wait, maybe it's the Breast
who's left? Stood up and sauntered off—*who*
       needs this shit?—and slammed the door shut behind her.
She's Elvis. She's *left the building.* Good

ol' young perky Elvis who was always leaving
         buildings, bodies. Not old, beaten-down, droopy-
                   booby Elvis
   who was busting seams and fist-
              pumping codeine. It's not
too difficult to imagine an all-shook-up Cell blue-suede shoeing
itself into Elvis, is it?

And why wouldn't it take over? Plant a flag in a soft
spot, invade an organ, call it *mine,* and salute? (Christ,

I'm using the "c-word" war rhetoric Kate hated, made me
swear no "lost her battle" bullshit in her obit and, I
tried, Kate, I did, but those girls of yours? I

had to say "survived by . . ." didn't I? It was
that or "left behind" and, God, you would never,
    never. And my boys? My three?)

Goddamnit. Let me begin again.

Dear Office Manager,

Please raise the temperature in your waiting room. Those of us who still
have nipples are painfully aware of them in these frigid, morgue-
cooler conditions. I don't mean to be insensitive, but we're already
shaking with self-talk, crossing our arms over our chests, thinking
of all we've rested on these breasts . . . the boys, the babies. And we're
counting the room, keeping score, doing the math. Maybe it's her. Maybe

it's me. Why wouldn't it be? Why *shouldn't* it be? One in eight, right? I don't
want it to be her; she's got pink hair, a husband who can't sit down. I've got
ten years on her, maybe 15. I went to Italy last spring; she's got
somebody at home who still sucks his thumb. Look, there's spit-up
on her shoulder. And speaking of spit and self-talk and shakes and stats,
morgue-cooler conditions and all this other hyper hyperbole shit, *please,*
for the love of God or Elvis or Kate or Pretty-in-Pink Punk Patient, *please,*
turn the air down and Fox News the fuck off.

EVEN THE DOG DOESN'T STAY ALIVE

Sometimes I find my legs wrapped around some
      man I knew years ago and never found particularly
         attractive   or one that just appeared like men do

         in books I don't read   or maybe it's that guy from high
    school   not the one I climbed into back seats for, but
the one I thought about when my boyfriend touched me   and

      we're never young again   it's all here and now   and   heat
                                        and   need
      and I'm not thinking about   my thighs   or condoms   or

ghosts of nuns who used to flatten themselves between me and the men
        I knew I didn't love until I silenced them   with want
or wine   and I don't know   exactly what's been said   that put

      me here   —usually in some bed I don't recognize or
        the top of a tile table I never would have believed

        would be sturdy enough— and it's light out   or
    it's not   and the room brims with   God, where have you been?   or
sighs with *Sure, why not*   and I'm in it, you know? Like *really* in it. Like

bad-love-songs-from-the-70s-Rod-Stewart *into* it
        like I-don't-notice-if-the-tile-is-cold into it   and then

and then   an awareness reaches out from within   and washes
             me cold   and I remember the man I usually wrap

      my legs around   and my mind thrums with *Jesus, how*
did I forget I'm married?   but my body shrugs   right now she
        truly doesn't give *one good goddamn shit* about some

promise I made 30 years ago   *you were just a kid,   it doesn't*
               even count   and how would he know?   oh, girl, why not?
               we're so close   why not   why not just   this once?

But we both know I might as well wake the fuck up   because I can't
               come back from where I've been   And my body?
       She's pissed.   Because it's always this way

               my head calling all the shots   my head a quicksand of killjoy
       my head a mine of memories I can't keep buried   my head
that brings the dog I loved best back from the dead   and then kills
       him all over again   my head

that left my dad on the porch
       to pour him another glass of wine   and my head
    that stilled and turned and formed the words

       Wait.   You won't be here when I come back, will you?   You're dead, right?
                       And my head that made my father nod and me wake
                               with tears tucked   into my throat.

           You know? *Fuck* my head.

But my mother   who always knew me best   came last night
           and I made her laugh   like only I could ever do   and it was
               the sound of the sky opening and the earth rushing up

                   and it was just as full and fierce as it always was
           and I stood in its shadow and warmed under it and then my head
           my fucking head said   *I can't believe I'll never hear you laugh again.*

And my mother said, "Oh, darlin'. You just did."

I'M JUST ANOTHER WHITE WOMAN PRACTICING YOGA

and there's a Buddha statue the color of mud in the corner
of the studio, but not in the center because, you know, Christians
live in this part of town and we all want the yoga experience—*give me*
serenity NOW! haha—but it's not like an altar, is it? And, sure, the lavender
candles are nice and the incense feels a little like college in the 80s when the smell
of weed seemed like something you should bury under your perm solution
while you slid into your Izod polo. And I love Jesus (and I like Buddha
fine, but not as much as Oprah), but either way, My Jesus doesn't hang out

at this studio—he gets lonely being the only brown guy—but
it's just as well, because the last time My Jesus came he couldn't stop
crying while I was doing the downward dog and, frankly, that's distracting
to all the other white women who are fighting hot flashes and teenage
kids who don't bother to light incense when they smoke their own weed
in their suburb houses that salute us as we drive our silver hybrids
into our two-car garages choking on lacrosse helmets and orange kayaks
and Costco cases of Mango Orange BodyArmor and . . . you know? I don't
want to talk about consumerism. I'm pretty sure that's not part
of the yoga "experience."

But I'm here on my hot pink mat with the orange peace symbols
and my grubby Groupon, because My Jesus is so much quieter than even
this yoga instructor and I like how she tells me there's no past or future, only
now   *breathe from your belly*   and I want that to be true, because people I love
keep dying   and my husband's job is being swallowed whole
and my favorite aunt had her last breast removed   and my favorite cousin
is on suicide watch which in Army-speak means he gets unlimited
refills on his prescriptions and an honorable discharge.

We move to Warrior Pose and she tells us the only enemy is fear, but
I think maybe she's just not on Twitter? A student called
me Woke As Fuck after a poetry reading last March and I
said, *Oh honey, you have no idea.* And maybe I said, *Thank you,* because

that's what white people do . . . we like to be congratulated
for noticing black boys keep dying with their hands in the air
while we keep talking about what they're doing with their knees

and we think it's admirable that we can imagine how a mama
might feel when there's a border between her and that baby she grew
under her heart and carried into a land that told her to "Give me
your tired and poor," but never mentioned we'll surround your daughter
with a chain link fence, throw her an Uncrustable, and wait six months
while we forget who she belongs to.   I'm working on balance

but it's hard to be a mountain when my son missed second period today
because he had to learn how to use a chair and a light switch to fight
off an AR-15. And I'm all about thoughts and prayers and finding
my center, but I have to remember to call Rubio again and tell him
we actually do give a shit about background checks no matter what the
goddamn NRA tells him. I'd like to settle into child's pose, but I have
to pee and I can't stop thinking about how *go back to where you came from*
is code for we liked it better when we didn't have to share our bathrooms.
And Ryan's still afraid to hold his boyfriend's hand in public and they're
so in love, it makes me cry   and if I could figure out who   and what
and how   I'd burn IT ALL to the fucking *ground*.   I'm pretty sure

I'm supposed to exhale now. My Jesus is waiting
for me in the car and it's 88 degrees at the end
of September and it's bad enough
the sea is melting
and the earth is in corpse
pose and we need a 16-year-old from Sweden to tell
us climate change isn't something we get
to believe in like Jesus or Buddha or even Oprah, but
right now   I'm so worried about my student Stefan down
at the prison who just can*not* keep insisting the COs treat
him like a human and he's back in solitary and there's no
air conditioning anywhere, but there's no
fan in The Box, either, only a window the size of a Bible,

and Stefan keeps passing out and sometimes the cockroaches
climb in his ears and it takes days before the nurse
pulls them out and sometimes they're still alive   and I'd
ask Buddha what I can do about any of this, but
he told us *Life is suffering* first   and if that isn't
the equivalent to *Bitch, please,* I don't what is.   I place

my forehead on the mat and it turns
out my son's in like with a girl who just might
like him back   and Terry just bought
her homeless student a bike   and
my husband made me a breakfast
burrito with veggie sausage and
I didn't even ask for it   and
a deer wandered into a cathedral
in France and stood in front
of the altar like he's the gift
he is   and it's Friday
morning and my dog
smells like rain and
my youngest son
just texted *Luv u*
and

the God in me recognizes
the God in you.

POSTFIX

ON GIVING YOURSELF PERMISSION AT 52

You pull wet poems out of your Midwest
childhood and hang them on the clothesline to dry
in a Florida sun. They drip onto the deck and burn

your dead mother's skin. You don't want to hurt
anyone, but the list of who's left keeps crumbling
in your hands and still your words wait. Somewhere

there's a baby crying. Your grandmother beat
your mother. Your mother beat herself. You slid
under her closed door, pressed your face to the glass

she rested under. You learned to wear socks
on wooden steps. Somewhere your grandmother
pours water in milk to make it stretch. The year before

he dies, your father tells you over white wine that you've
changed. It seems you used to say *I see your point.* It seems
you used to not *take some topics so personally.* It seems

your father liked you better before. Somewhere
in a cemetery, a daughter rests her cheek on a headstone.
One son tells you not to use his name, another

wants to know what you're afraid of, a third says his friend's
mom *always puts* her *children first.* Somewhere a mother lowers
the hem to her skirt. Your student writes about truth

and her ink stains your hands. Somewhere a little girl breaks
the night with a scream. Your poems wait on the line
while you put skin onto bones. Night is coming.

Oh, girl, it is always, always coming.

ACKNOWLEDGMENTS & NOTES

A special thank you to the editors of the following journals where these poems first appeared in various forms.

The Grief Diaries: "It's Been a Couple of Crappy Years," "Dear Facebook (for Hire) Quiz Writer," "My Father Learns to Say I Love You Before He Dies," "Misplaced"

Juxtaprose: "Mattel, in Their Infinite Wisdom, Decides Sally Ride Would Want Makeup"

The Missouri Review: Poem of the Week: "My Son Tells Me He's Thinking of Joining the Military" (originally "It May Be")

Literary Mama: "A Prayer for My 17-Year-Old Son on the Other Side of the Door"

NELLE: "Cloud Cover"

Pretty Owl Poetry: "A Student Wonders Why I Started Writing Poetry in My 40s," "I Thought I'd Teach My Poem to Play Guitar," and "Even the Dog Stays Dead"

Rattle: "To My Student with the Dime-Sized Bruises on the Back of Her Arms Who's Still on Her Cell Phone"

The Sun: "It's Friday Afternoon in a Florida State Penitentiary and the Men Read Poetry"

Superstition Review: "Bathing Your Mother: A Beginner's Guide," "Depression, Mom's"

Without a Doubt: Poems Illuminating Faith (anthology published by New York Quarterly); "A Prayer for My 17-Year-Old Son on the Other Side of the Door"

Notes

"I Thought I'd Teach My Poem to Play Guitar" is in appreciation of Marge Piercy's "A Work of Artifice"

"It's a Friday Afternoon in a Florida Penitentiary and the Men Read Poetry": Poems read during this class:

"The Whipping" by Robert Hayden
"Still I Rise" by Maya Angelou
"If You Forget Me" by Pablo Neruda
"First Kiss" by Tim Seibles

WITH GRATITUDE

The love and support I've received from so many is truly an embarrassment of riches. I'd like to extend a special thanks . . .

To my mother who taught me to love poetry and my father who always encouraged me (and would have discouraged much of the language in this collection). I miss you both more than I can say.

To my amazing (and patient!) editor Courtney LeBlanc and Riot in Your Throat who took this manuscript out of the sludge pile and gave it a home. I'm honored and humbled to be part of this family.

To the poets who took me under their angel wings and blessed me real good with their words and wisdom, especially Joy Harjo, Russ Kesler, Lia Purpura, and Katie Riegel.

To my "Litlando" writer friends who inspire and encourage me: Susan Fallows, Nathan Holic, Chrissy Kolaya, David James Poissant, and Ryan Rivas.

To Marco and the other men I write with on Fridays at a state penitentiary, especially James, Dwayne, Julio, and Eddie. Thank you for sharing your stories with me. And, Marco? Look! I'm writing something positive! Thank you for always reminding me to choose joy.

To all of the students I've been blessed with over the years. You taught me more than I taught you. Sending a little extra love to Sean Ironman, Emma Reinhardt, Helene Brun, and Malcolm Kelly. (And a special hug to "my" English class in Schleswig, Germany. Moin, moin, y'all.)

To my extended family—especially Katie Carbone, John Bland, and Kay Barlow who read my work and ask for more—and my sister, Regina Jackman, who always remembers me with a notebook. I'm sorry you had to sit through so many of my "readings" when we were kids, but thanks for being such a great audience. Hugs to my nieces Katrina Jackman and Samantha Uttich, and to my super supportive mother-in-law Rosalie Uttich.

To Mark Pursell who knows me too well and tells me I'm ridiculous just when I need him to. I adore you.

To my circle of women friends, especially Michele Alonso, Terry Arya, Kristen Denny, Tish Haynes, Michelle Hidalgo, Janet Hynes, Heather Konrardy, Stacy Marsteller, Kimberly Menard, and Nicole Pendleton. Thank you all for filling me up. Also, thanks to my college roomies: Jacki Brunk, Tina Colgan, and Sara Rogan. Thank you for asking me to read my stories to you all . . . and for not rolling your eyes when I walked around in a flannel shirt and called it my "writing outfit."

To Ryan Skaryd who fills my life with joy and crystals. Thank you for all the times you read this collection and came over with color-coded Post-Its and sparkling water. I can't do life without you.

To Terry Ann Thaxton, a brilliant poet and an even better friend. Thank you for always telling me I'm brave and actually a "real" poet, even if I haven't been fully convinced yet.

To Debbie Piercefield, editor extraordinaire, who wanted this book published more than I did and dedicated countless hours reading the work and talking me off the ledge. Everyone should be blessed with a friend like you. There wouldn't be a book without you.

To my soul sis, Leticia R. Uttich, who created the art for the cover of this collection and who models passion and purpose every day. I want to be you when I grow up.

To my sons, Jake, Zack, and Cody. I won the lottery being your mom. Thank you for all the ways you love me and all the ways you make me laugh. I'm so proud of the men you've become.

And, of course, to my main squeeze, Kevin, who keeps me fed and somewhat sane. I can't think of anything you wouldn't do for me and, God, what a gift that is 30-something years in. I'm so glad I said yes all those years ago under a Boulder sky.

And, finally, to you, the person who picked up this book and took it home. Thank you, thank you, thank you.

ABOUT THE AUTHOR

Laurie Rachkus Uttich is the author of the poetry collection, *Somewhere, a Woman Lowers the Hem of Her Skirt* (Riot in Your Throat Press, 2022). Laurie's prose and poetry have been published in *Brevity*; *Creative Nonfiction*; *Fourth Genre*; *Iron Horse Literary Review*; *JuxtaProse*; *The Missouri Review: Poem of the Week*; *Poets and Writers*; *Rattle*; *River Teeth*; *Ruminate*; *Split Lip Magazine*; *The Sun*; *Superstition Review*; *Sweet: A Literary Confection*; *Terrain.org*; and others. Laurie grew up in the Midwest and now lives in Orlando. She teaches at the University of Central Florida where she occasionally sneaks her dog into the classroom. Visit her at www.laurieuttich.com.

ABOUT THE PRESS

Riot in Your Throat is an independent press that publishes fierce, feminist poetry.

Support independent authors, artists, and presses.

Visit us online:
www.riotinyourthroat.com

CPSIA information can be obtained
at www.ICGtesting.com
Printed in the USA
BVHW011601210422
634952BV00014BA/503